Designing with Concrete

Karen Keyes

Keyes, LLC

KEYES

Copyright © 2021 Karen Keyes

All rights reserved

No part of this book may be reproduced, or stored in a retrieval system, or transmitted in any form or by any means, electronic, mechanical, photocopying, recording, or otherwise, without express written permission of the publisher.

Printed in the United States of America

This book is dedicated to my parents and my family.

Thank you to my parents who taught me how to work hard and have a passion for what I do. Thank you for all of the life and work lessons.

*Thank you to my husband, Jeff Keyes,
and four kids: Evelyn, Audrey, Ben and Caleb.
You are my world!*

Contents

Title Page

Copyright

Dedication

Introduction

Step 1 - Determine Your Budget	1
Step 2 - Determine Grading	3
Step 3 - Determine Layout	6
Step 4 - Consider your surroundings	8
Step 5 - Identify the function	10
Step 6 - Identify concerns and desires	12
Step 7 - Desired maintenance	22
Step 8 - Jointing	24
Step 9 - Color	28
Step 10 - Textures	40
Step 11: Finding a Qualified Contractor	49
Conclusion	52
About The Author	55

Introduction

Who cares about concrete? It's gray, it's hard, and it cracks. Oh, but there is so much more! Yes, it can weave paths in and out of parks, it can provide a smooth surface for kids to ride their bikes on, and it can be a place homeowners can display their cool new patio furniture without sinking into the grass. But, what if we took it to the next level? What if we could take that hard and utilitarian surface and tie in the design, the setting, and the purpose in an aesthetically pleasing manner? Concrete is more than functional. Concrete is art. Concrete can be colored, molded, and transformed into many purposes.

While attending a seminar, I mentioned to someone I worked in decorative concrete; all they could imagine was concrete countertops. While concrete countertops can be artful, there is so much more to using concrete as an artistic medium. A sidewalk can be transformed into an art piece. Sure, not everyone walking across the beautifully colored and sandy concrete path will say, "wow! what an awesome piece of art!", but it should be designed and crafted with artistic care and passion. Art isn't always about the wow factor, but about bringing people together and creating peaceful environments. If a sidewalk can link people and places together and do it in a calming matter I would consider it a piece of the artful landscape.

I hope you find this resource useful when tackling your next exterior decorative concrete project. I grew up in decorative concrete and I live and breathe it every day. It's an exciting medium with enormous design potential. Designing with decorative concrete can be an appealing yet daunting task. There are thousands of possibilities if you have a decent decorative concrete contractor nearby. So where does one begin? This guide will help you through some of the crucial factors to think about and the hoops to jump through before any of the "mud" (concrete lingo for wet concrete) hits the ground. This is not a technical document but an idea book meant to inspire, inform and intrigue.

With every construction project, I recommend having a good team to support you and help you follow the rules. Not included in these steps are some of the crucial safety steps you need to consider before doing any type of project. Please locate any wires or utilities before digging. Also check out your overhead conditions and hazards. Check with your local jurisdiction for any permit and inspection requirements. And always wear proper safety attire. When in doubt, hire a professional. Also before anything, have a realistic budget in mind before jumping into the project. Details such as access, thickness of concrete, sub-grade requirements, reinforcement, radial forming, and steps can all have major impact on your budget.

The industry of decorative concrete continues to evolve. With great landscape architects and contractors, new possibilities are discovered on a regular basis.

Starting with a rough idea of what you want to spend on the project, you will need to be prepared adjust your expectations as we progress through the design considerations. We will explore the 11 steps together, and most of the fun and first artistic steps don't actually come until step 8, but you need to get through the first 7 steps to have a successful project you can enjoy for years to come.

The steps are:
1. Determine your budget
2. Determine grading
3. Determine layout
4. Consider your surroundings
5. Identify function

6. Identify concerns and desires
7. Think about your desired maintenance
8. Jointing
9. Color
10. Textures
11. Finding your contractor

So get out your idea book and sketch pad and let's begin!

Step 1 - Determine Your Budget

I already briefly mentioned this, but the most crucial step before dreaming up your next hardscaping project is to determine your budget. Now, this is a bit difficult to finalize before you do the rest of the steps in this book, but you need to know how much money you are willing to contribute to the project. Establishing a budget will help in some of the decision making process throughout the entire project. Throughout this book, I will have a call out box for items that may impact your budget. Some may be out of your control. Others will enable you to choose your priorities when working through the ideas of your project.

For a frame of reference, most qualified contractors in my region cannot do anything for less than $2,500 (the mere cost of starting up the trucks and paying the craftsmen to come to your site). And once you reach 1,000 square feet or more, the most basic upgraded concrete can still be around $10 per square foot and go up from there. Setting realistic expectations from the beginning on what

KAREN KEYES

your project could potentially cost will give you more design freedom and awareness. All costs fluctuate on a regular basis, so do check with your local contractor for current and local prices for your project.

Step 2 - Determine Grading

Before you pour any concrete, grading needs to be determined. This can be fairly simple if you are working on a project with pre-determined grades. However, some projects are more complex and you will need to bring in a civil engineer to determine the best grading for drainage and accessibility issues. But, in this step, I will offer some tips and guidelines to get you started. First, be sure the concrete you are placing will slope away from any buildings. You don't want water gushing into the building or home after a rain storm, do you?

Sloping away from the foundation will not only save you from potential flooding, it will also help protect your foundation from any undeserved settling or deterioration. You may also need a soils report to help determine if the ground you are working on is

BUDGET IMPACTS:
- Importing or exporting dirt, sand and rock
- Drains
- Geotechnical engineer soil reports

sound for your new concrete slab, or if you'll need to take out some of the material and replace it with more stable material.

In addition to sloping the concrete away from any structures, you may need to consider a drainage plan. I worked on a back patio once where the home owner had the rain falling off her roof onto the patio, but the patio was enclosed by a beautiful wall. It looked gorgeous when dry, but with every rainstorm, she had a pool on her back patio. Some people pay extra for backyard pools, but this one was causing damage to her home and made outdoor entertainment challenging. So, we tore out all of the existing concrete; we installed new trench drains which ran all along the back retaining wall facing her garden; then we replaced the concrete to slope to these new trench drains. We also tied the gutters and downspouts into the same drainage system. Now, every time it rains, the water flows over the surface and right into the new drainage system. The homeowner no longer has the concern and liability of the standing water on her back patio.

Too much grading can be a concern as well. For commercial projects, ADA regulations need to be taken into careful consideration, and they are good rules of thumb for every concrete grading plan. The maximum cross slope is 2%. Any more than 2% and the paving is non-ADA compliant; it's also awkward to walk across and unsafe. But remember, you do need some slope for proper drainage and to avoid pooling. There is a fine balance and grading is an important first step to your concrete project not to skip.

Grading can add interesting design elements to a project. The grading of a site may require retaining walls or steps. Both walls and steps add new design possibilities to a project. They can be utilitarian or decorative. Lights can be added into walls and steps, they can be straight or radius, and can be finished to match or complement the surrounding paving. Differing heights and elevations in an exterior space adds interest and a new dynamic to a design which may be challenging, but the end results can be stunning.

Many of the finishes we will discuss later on can be applied to vertical surfaces as well as horizontal. Remember, decorative concrete is not always just for flat surfaces. If you need walls or steps in your project, there are creative and aesthetically pleasing methods of tying them into your overall design.

Step 3 - Determine Layout

Layout goes hand-in-hand with grading.

> **BUDGET IMPACTS:**
> - Stairs
> - Radiuses - whether in steps, walls, or concrete forming - radiuses cost more in material and labor to form and finish.
> - Finishing the vertical face of anything costs more money
> - Railings
> - Fences
> - Walls

Without proper layout, a grading plan cannot work; and vice versa. However, layout can start getting into the exciting design aspect. Think about where the grading may require steps, ramps, railings, walls, and any other features due to the site complexities. Sometimes the grading and design will require a thickened edge (not quite a step, but also not flush with the surrounding finishes).

Sometimes you will need steps to help achieve a drastic grade change. Other times a retaining wall will be needed to hold back part of the land and showcase the new decorative concrete space. With these elements you can start to determine other layout options. Do you want all straight edges or would you like some radiuses? How long do you want the steps? Where will the railings or other safety features go? Where do you want the hard surfaces? Layout is the roadmap to the spacial design.

Step 4 - Consider your surroundings

Whether new or existing construction, paying special attention to what is going on next to the concrete is just as important as installing the concrete itself.

For example, if you are placing concrete next to sod, do you want it to be flush with the grass or a step up from it? Or, if you are placing concrete next to a building, in addition to sloping away from it, think about the landings and the spaces that it is creating.

> **BUDGET IMPACTS:**
> - Irrigation replacement or changes
> - Landscaping
> - Drains
> - Access
>   - Demolition
>   - Equipment
>   - Concrete truck or pump

The same resident who had the unplanned backyard pool for her patio, also had concerns about her back door. When her grandkids came over, they would run up a steep staircase from the driveway to the back door. This back door also was the gateway to their back patio. But, before we came in, it was a tiny three feet wide by three feet long stoop… and the screen door swung out towards the staircase … so if a kid or guest was unlucky, the door could smack them right in the face and send them tumbling back down the steep staircase to the driveway. Not an ideal situation, and a definite concern for these grandparents. So by considering our surroundings, we had to go back to step two of the planning process and adjust our layout. Because the door swings out, the stairs needed to come up to the landing, and additional stairs needed to lead to the back patio, so creative layout adjusting was required. We ended up enlarging the stoop and extending the steps a bit further away from the landing. Now both points of access for the door provide enough clearance to safely welcome guests of all ages.

But buildings and safety concerns are not the only surroundings to consider. Landscaping can be another huge consideration. If you are working on a renovation, you need to determine the best route of access for the concrete construction, how your existing irrigation may be affected, as well as how to protect the adjacent landscaping. Landscaping can also affect the concrete. In Colorado, I often see the beautiful quaking Aspen trees turning the surrounding concrete black when the leaves fall from the tree. I also see old trees with roots pushing up old sidewalks. I love trees and honestly think a concrete project is not complete until it is fully landscaped, but you do need to consider the effects of nearby plant life. If it's a renovation, you will also want to develop a plan to protect the plant life as much as reasonably possible. Large tree roots can cause future concrete heaving as well.

Other surroundings that may come into play are pools, other paving materials, mulch, etc. If you are planning a new pool deck, remember any material you choose should be rinsed down after exposure to the pool chemicals to minimize whiting of the surface.

Step 5 - Identify the function

Sometimes when the phone rings, someone just wants a slab so the muddy dogs have some place dry to walk over before running back into the house. Or they may just want a sturdy place to set a shed or a hot tub. If all they want is concrete, decorative doesn't really make sense. But function plays a big role in the design of decorative concrete.

BUDGET IMPACTS:
- Concrete finishes
- Textures
- Colors
- Custom elements

For example, a pool deck will require different considerations than a meditation path. Think about the people who will be using the space and start to identify some traits of those people and what types of concrete needs may be required by those people. For example, if you have a splash pad in a park for a family with children and grandparents, you will want to make sure you choose a finish which is gentle on the feet, but also provides enough traction to minimize slipping. If you are paving a path for a retirement community, you may want even more traction to minimize liability of slip and falls, but you also have to be wary of trip hazards.

Step 6 - Identify concerns and desires

With identifying function comes a new list: concerns and desires. Let's take the pool deck example. If you are creating a pool deck for a family of all ages, your list of concerns or desires may look something like this:

- Traction - can't be too slippery
- Heat - can't be too hot to walk across in the summer time
- Brightness - although I don't want it too hot, I also don't want it to be too bright so I need sunglasses on just to look at it
- Comfort - can't be too rough on bare feet
- Aesthetics - we want it to look nice
- Coordination - we want it to look nice with the pool tile, coping, and house finishes

Details to think about when writing out your list of concerns and desires can include:

- Traction

DESIGNING WITH CONCRETE

- Age of audience
- Color
- Solar reflectance
- Drainage
- Trees and landscaping
- Maintenance
- Longevity
- Aesthetics
- Trends
- Reinforcement needs and concrete strength
- Sealer

> **BUDGET IMPACTS:**
> - Added grip to sealers is an added upfront and maintenance cost
> - Concrete finishes vary in costs
> - Concrete colors vary in costs
> - Some finishes require different maintenance than others

Traction:

Not all finishes are created equal as we will discuss later on. But when it comes to slipperiness, some finishes are more slippery than others. Smooth troweled concrete is not recommended in areas where slipperiness is a concern on the exterior. Some stamped concrete can be slippery because the texture on the surface is stamped nice and smooth to relocate the surface of stone. While beautiful, if can be slippery. When looking at stamped concrete in an area where slipperiness may be a concern (driveway, pool deck, patio for kids running through sprinklers), ask for a mock up or visit an installation of the same pattern and stamp. Some stamp patterns have fine traction while others are more slippery. It depends on the final finish surface and the pattern of the stamp. Directional broom finish can cause some directional slip concerns and some broom finishes wear down quickly. Exposed aggregates provide good traction, however I wouldn't recommend a coarse exposed aggregate where people will be barefoot or in a park where kids could trip and fall. I would recommend more of a sand exposed finish in those settings. There is always an option to add grit to a sealer to add more traction to a surface if you do like a smoother finish, but that would need to be re-applied routinely to maintain its traction.

Age of Audience:

As I eluded to above, both young and old have needs when it comes to concrete. Kids can trip and fall and skin their knees. If running through sprinklers or playing on a splash pad, a finish with some traction but not too rough is desired. The elderly have similar slipping concerns, but also take into consideration accessibility concerns. Some concrete patterns are too rough for walkers and nimble feet to shuffle across.

Color:

Identifying your range of color will help identify your budget and finish options. The more natural colors are usually more affordable. Whereas vibrant colors require a little more creativity on how to achieve. Standard gray concrete can beautiful as well with great finishing and detail techniques.

Solar Reflectance:

On LEED projects and sustainable projects looking for higher SRI (solar reflective index), choosing lighter colors can help achieve some of those goals. The higher the solar reflectance the less the heat is absorbed is to the surface. Not only is this important for our planet, but its more friendly on bare feet and potentially the concrete's adjacent surrounds.

Drainage:

As mentioned in the grading section, there needs to be a plan for storm water management. There are some creative solutions for drainage that go beyond just slope and drains. There are a few pervious solutions as well. There is the traditional pervious concrete - which has its pros and cons. It is tricky to install correctly in many climates and is not the most decorative finish. There are ways to extend sawcuts below the concrete slab into an underground drainage system. My personal favorite pervious concrete solution is a continuously reinforced open grid paving system. The voids in this system allow for flexibility to sod over, seed, plant individual plants, or simply fill with crushed rock.

Another simple solution is to create gaps between slabs and fill those gaps with pervious material as well, such as herbs, grass, mulch or decorative rocks.

Trees and landscaping:

As mentioned earlier, concrete looks better with both furnishings and landscaping. When planning for your concrete, look around to see if there is existing landscaping that needs to be protected or kept in mind. Mature trees or even growing trees can have an impact on your potential design. We've all walked through town going up and down on the sidewalk like a rollercoaster because tree roots pushed the sidewalk up. Plan your concrete with your landscaping in mind. The concrete should be just a part of the plan. A good landscape architect can see and plan for all elements of the design and can come up with creative and functional solutions.

Longevity:

Well constructed concrete should last a long time, however some people want a quicker fix. Toppings could be a solution to coat an existing slab to make it look better, but nothing lasts longer than a well constructed concrete slab. If it is a more temporary slab, things like color, finish, or even concrete strength may not be as important to you.

Aesthetics:

I love decorative concrete, so the aesthetics are always important to me. However, there is a time and place for decorative concrete, and not all applications need to be decorative. I worked on a retail center once and they had grand dreams for decorative concrete across the entire site. However, they quickly discovered that their budget could not support such big dreams. So, we worked together to identify the key focal points where decorative concrete was most important: store entries, plazas and cross walks. Some of the sidewalks between the stores did not need to be decorative, and definitely the back-of-house concrete pads could just be utilitarian. As much as I would love to see all concrete to have some element of enhancement, it certainly is not necessary everywhere.

Trends:

Yes, just like the fashion world, the concrete world has trends as well. In Colorado, stamped concrete took off in the 80's and 90's and then tapered off. In other parts of the country it is still a very trendy finish. In Colorado light sand finishes are the current trend while it is just emerging in other parts of the country. There are trends in colors as well. Currently I am seeing a trend in different shades of gray with a mix of some very vibrant colors - depending on the application. Where reds and tans were popular not too long ago. Some trends are timeless while some can fade. When choosing your decorative concrete think about if you would still like it in five or ten years.

Reinforcement and Concrete Strength

In my opinion all concrete should have some level of reinforcement. ACI and geotechnical engineers are the experts on the technical requirements of concrete reinforcement and strength, but I do want to touch on it briefly. I recommend using some version of stealth micro fibers in all decorative concrete. Why the stealth version? I don't like hairy concrete. Normal fibers will be seen on a decorative finish and will either leave your surface hairy (they may eventually wear off) or need to be burned off (not very eco-friendly). Fibers are important for the initial curing. They are not for long term reinforcement. They help keep the concrete together during at the very beginning of their life in the concrete - they help minimize shrinkage cracking and help retain some moisture through the entire slab to help maintain a nice even cure.

In addition to fibers, steel or fiber bar reinforcement can be used. If there is a chance your soils may settle here or there, they I recommend steel reinforcement. You can get rebar or wire mesh. The steel helps hold the slab together, so if the ground moves, the slab stays together. Dowels are important between pours and structures as well. Dowels are either short pieces of rebar or a diamond-shaped piece of steel - both with the intention of keeping the pieces together. The dowel bars, when inserted into a sleeve - will allow some movement back and forth, but not up and down. Concrete does contract as it cures, so you want some ability for it to move from side-to-side, but you don't want it to move up and down where it could cause trippers, or worse, make it impossible for a door to open! The diamond-shaped dowel works similarly, it also gets put into a sleeve and allows slight back and forth movement - the diamond-shaped dowel systems work best on radius's since the movement isn't in a perpendicular line. If you do have shifting soils, the sub-grade is also crucial. This may require some exporting of your existing sub-grade and importing of some stronger material or road base. The sub-base should be compacted.

DESIGNING WITH CONCRETE

For exterior concrete strength, regionally I prefer 4,000-5,000 psi depending on the recommendations from the engineer. The happy medium for me is 4500 psi. 5000 is a little trickier to finish with many of the decorative finishes, but it holds up better in Colorado's climate and the inevitable use of some deciders (which is a big no-no on any concrete; deicers almost always cause surface spalling). 4,000 psi is a good strong mix, but I bump it up if I know it will be used by a municipality and get heavy traffic and use.

Sealer

The concrete industry has many sealers. I recommend you lean on the advise of your contractor to dial in the perfect one for your application However, to help guide the selection process, think about what purpose you want the sealer to have. I recommend sealing all new concrete to help protect it and get it through its first year of life so that it has the best chance to survive many years to come. There are penetrating sealers that penetrate into the concrete surface. There are sealers that create a protective layer on top of the concrete. And there are many sealers in between. In a porte-cochere or driveway, I would guide people towards selecting something that repels stains at the surface, knowing that stains from cars may not get washed off right away. For a splash pad or an area that will see water frequently, I prefer something that penetrates into the concrete a bit more and doesn't create a slippery membrane. There are glossy options and matte options. Some sealers can boost colored concrete's vibrancy while others simply seal the concrete without making a statement. Understand that you have choices when it comes to concrete sealers and it is important to seal concrete. If you are unsure whether or not your concrete is sealed, a good test is to pour some water on the slab, if it beads up on the surface - it is sealed.

DESIGNING WITH CONCRETE

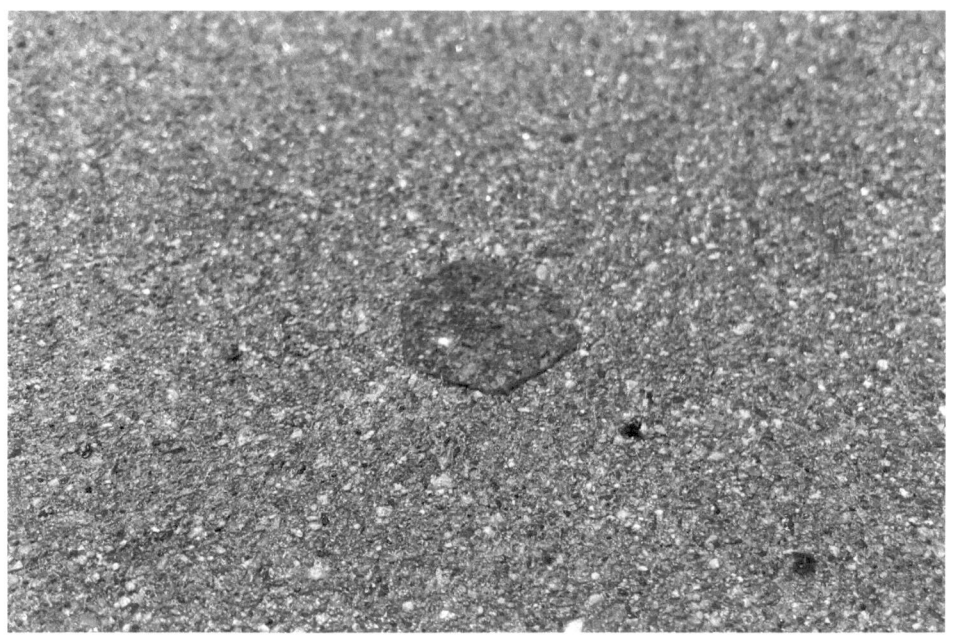

Step 7 - Desired maintenance

I mentioned this in step five, because it can be a concern or a desire. A common misconception is that concrete is a no maintenance option. Unfortunately, there is no such thing as no maintenance. At the very least, you will need to keep it clean. But before you start picking out colors and finishes, you do need to decide how much time you want to commit to maintaining your new decorative concrete. Whether it is reapplying a sealer or stains, pressure washing off sap, or re-caulking of the expansion joints along your house to keep the moisture out, all concrete requires some degree of maintenance.

> **BUDGET IMPACTS:**
> - Resealing
> - Caulking
> - Cleaning
> - Staining

I have visited many old stamped concrete projects where the owner complains that the color is gone or faded, where it truly just needs a good clean and seal to make the color pop again. Identify early on what you are willing to commit to maintaining your concrete slab.

Step 8 - Jointing

People who think concrete doesn't need any joints are either pouring a 3-foot slab, or just haven't been educated on the basics of concrete. All concrete cracks, but it is the job of the designer and concrete contractor to take steps to minimize the cracking. There are three types of joints I would like to address:
1. Isolation joints
2. Contraction joints
3. Decorative joints

First, isolation joints are your gridline for success. Isolation joints help protect the concrete from the effects of concrete expansion and contraction while it sets. After you place a concrete slab, moisture starts to evaporate and the concrete mass you just placed shrinks slightly and the chemistry of the concrete mixture can also make it expand while it sets. If you are placing concrete against a house, columns, walls, planters, another concrete slab, you will want to place an isolation joint. Isolation, or sometimes referred to as expansion joints, are made of a flexible material such as foam or asphalt to help compress to the movement of the slab. The material can handle some pressure and strain of the moving concrete much better than a rigid material (such as a building). Typically I like to see some sort of removable cap on the expansion joint material, because when your decorative concrete is finished, it can be removed and sealed up with a caulking material to prevent additional moisture from seeping in or weeds taking root in the joint.

> **BUDGET IMPACTS:**
> - Caulking of expansion joints. Costs upfront and needs to be maintained, but can save you expenses in the future
> - Decorative cuts
> - Beveled cuts add an extra step, so extra money

Second, contraction joints serve the purpose of minimizing cracking. Concrete cracks like to take the path of least resistance. Let's say you have a building corner with concrete surrounding the corner. If you don't have a control joint at the corner, I can almost guarantee you will have a crack. One way to minimize cracking is to create square shapes at the edges and corners. A rule of thumb for the thickness of a contraction/control joint is to do minimum of 1/4 the thickness of the slab when cutting your control joints. For spacing, you will want a maximum of 30 times the depth of the slab. For example, if you have a 4" slab it would look like: 4" x 30 = 120". In that instance, you would have a maximum of 10' spacing for contraction joints. For a long stretch of sidewalk, you would want a joint at least every 5 feet or so. There are always exceptions to this rule depending on slab layout, but these are good general rules of thumb.

Third, and probably the most exciting, decorative cuts can add great design potential. Even a boring old gray concrete slab can get pretty fancy with decorative scoring. Once you have your expansion and control joints laid out, play with the pattern and choose where you can add pizzaz with decorative scoring. Decorative sawcuts can be strait or radius; they can create banding; they can create way finding; they can mimic nearby architecture lines; or they can simply add a bit of symmetry.

And, sawcuts do not have to be the standard 1/8" cut. I have seen beautiful slabs with a nice beveled cut to create more of a tile appearance. The bevel cut also allows for a cleaner cut by opening up the sawcut and minimizing the weak edge which likes to ravel. Decorative sawcuts can be any depth you like, because they are just for decorative purposes. Some people like the shadows a deep cut produces, while others prefer a shallow cut because they don't want to have to worry about keeping it clean. I would recommend cutting your decorative cuts after the 28-day cure time frame, especially if you plan on creating any dead-end, or T-joints. When a cut ends abruptly at a perpendicular joint, it has the tendency to want to keep on going. If the concrete isn't fully cured and you have a dead-end joint, you will most likely have a crack there within 30 days because the concrete will want to continue that joint. Because these cuts are purely decorative they do not have to be as deep as control joints, and where they meet an edge, they will be more shallow because of the circular nature of the saw.

DESIGNING WITH CONCRETE

Step 9 - Color

Color is by far my favorite topic. And when it comes to concrete there are countless ways to color concrete. Let's start with the basics.

> **BUDGET IMPACTS:**
> - White Cement
> - Dark colors
> - Exotic colors
> - Custom colors
> - Integral color
> - Custom aggregates
> - Aggregate exposure
> - Maintenance costs of stains and paints - they will not last forever and will need to be restored if you want to keep the color

DESIGNING WITH CONCRETE

Cement

This one is simple. Cement usual comes in your choice of gray cement or white cement. Gray comes standard and all ready mix supplies will be able to easily supply it for you. White cement is usually available, but you will pay a premium for it since it usually requires a different bin at the plant, it will require the truck to be thoroughly cleaned out before and after mixing it, and it finishes differently than gray cement, so the labor to install will be higher. Some regions do not have white cement as an option at the ready-mix plants, so be aware of local availability. Also be aware that concrete looks different from batch to batch There will be slight variations between loads, especially concrete poured on different days. A environmental factors as well as batching processes can have an impact on how concrete comes out. Also, freshly poured concrete will look different than concrete poured last week.

Integral color

This is the next step up from your traditional every day concrete. Integral color comes in many standard natural shades of browns, reds, and grays. Remember, you are typically adding these colors to a gray base, so if you start with gray, you cannot get lighter than that without some additional chemistry or costs. There are also some premium colors which you will pay a premium for that may or may not be worth the extra cost (for example, blue concrete). Integral color is mixed in the concrete truck with the cement. It is pigment that is added to the concrete and is an integral part of the concrete. The benefit of an integral color is that it is through the entire mix. If you chip or wear down the surface, you will still have the color. From a cost standpoint, the more pigment required to make a color, the more expensive. You may see several shades of the same color on a color chart, the lightest of the shades is the cheapest, the darkest is the most expensive. There is a carbon black used to make some black or dark gray colors, be mindful that it is not UV stable and should not be used outside. There are some alternatives to achieve the darker colors, but be aware of certain limitations and cost implications of such dark colors.

Color hardener

Traditionally seen with stamped concrete, color hardeners are a cement and pigment powder that is broadcasted to the surface of wet cement and worked into the surface. With stamped concrete, concrete is placed, color hardener is thrown across the surface and troweled in, then a release agent is spread across the surface to create a clean release of the stamp texture and a shadowing effect if it is a tinted release agent. As the name implies, a color hardener hardens the surface while adding color. Because it is added to the concrete during the finishing stage, it is part of the concrete slab and more durable than a stain or dye added after the concrete cures.

What I absolutely love about color hardeners is the design possibilities and color potential. When a bright blue or white may not have been in your budget initially, it may be possible with a color hardener. Since a color hardener is only on the surface, you are not paying for inches of the color beneath the surface. Now, if it chips or wears down (more likely in a vehicular setting), you will see gray, so that is a downside. But, if you want 5 crazy colors in a 10 feet wide by 10 feet long concrete slab, you can actually achieve it with a single load of concrete. Not only will you save on forming costs, short load fees, and 5 different integral color costs, you will also have a more structurally sound piece of concrete! When the concrete is poured monolithically, you are minimizing the stress points for the concrete wanting to crack.

Stain

There are many types of concrete stains, dyes, tinted sealers and paints out there. For purely coloring exterior concrete, you will get the longest life out of an integral color. If looking to color a large area, stain is not the best choice if a similar color is achievable with integral color or color hardeners. Stains and dyes are surface-applied and may fade or wear off of horizontal surfaces if not maintained regularly. I would recommend a reactive stain on a sand exposed finish if you want it to last more than a year. Stains color the cement in the concrete mix. On an exposed finish, the sand or rocks are on the wear surface, so the stained cement lies protected just below that. If you use a stain outside, make sure it is UV stable and have it sealed. I recommend stain for coloring accent areas or to create art on concrete. Stain can create dramatic or subtle differences in a slab and can create interest in an otherwise plain piece of concrete. It can be applied to 20-year-old concrete or 20-day-old concrete.

There are a few choices when it comes to stain:

> **Reactive acid stain**:
> The traditional is a reactive acid stain. This comes in only about 9 different colors. Reactive stains use chemistry to

color the concrete, the components of the stain react with the components of the concrete. They are a bit unpredictable, but they can create stunning results and I believe they penetrate a bit deeper into the surface because of that reaction. They do need to be neutralized and they should be sealed. It is tough to get a uniform color across a large area with these stains, but they are great for creating organic masterpieces.

Water-based stains and dyes:
These are stains that have been crafted to stain concrete and are a bit more predictable. What you see is what you get, whereas an acid stain may look orange when you put it down but can come out blue. Water-based stains have a larger variety of color and are more consistent than reactive stains. They are translucent as well, so if you are working with a gray cement base the color will look different than if you are working with a white cement base.

Tinted sealers and paint:
There are solid colored sealers that can color concrete as well. They are more comparable to paint in my option because they are not translucent. You will cover of the color of the concrete completely. These do not work well on exposed finishes where you want to see the sand or rock. They are very flat in color unless you layer different colors on top of each other. There are creative ways to make these work very well, and there are great instances when these are appropriate, but they would not be my go-to for coloring concrete since it covers up the character of the concrete and they will require maintenance to keep the color lasting.

Toppings

Another way to color concrete is to apply a thin topping over the surface to accent an area or dress up an existing slab. This is a great alternate to stains or dyes as you can get more vibrant and durable colors. Similar to many tinted sealers or paints, it will cover up the existing concrete completely. The technology of concrete toppings has evolved over the years, allowing for more versatility in colors and finishes. Just like with traditional concrete, toppings can be stamped, troweled, broomed and exposed.

Toppings can go on as thin as the thickness of the credit card and can be feathered to adjacent surface elevations, making it an ideal enhancement for some renovation. When choosing a topping versus a full depth replacement, look at the condition of the existing surface. If it is in decent shape and has tricky construction access, a topping is a good choice. However, if the concrete requires a lot of repairs before a topping can be placed, then consider a complete removal and replacement for the best possible outcome. If concrete is heaving, spalling, or has visible structural problems, it is most likely not a good candidate for a topping. A topping is only as good as the surface beneath it - if the surface beneath it has failures, the topping will fail.

DESIGNING WITH CONCRETE

Aggregates

We will get into textures in the next chapter, but the trends in the industry are strongly leaning on the exposed aggregate finish. The most popular in Colorado is sand finish, but many other exposed aggregates are re-gaining popularity as designers see the possibilities of color within the aggregate. Where you are located may drive your exposed aggregate decisions. In Colorado we are blessed with beautiful natural river aggregates that our ready-mix plants already use every day. By exposing just the sand, or even the rock, new dimensions in color emerge even from plain gray concrete. By adding pigment to that you can create new subtle tones, but when you are feeling extra adventurous you can mix up the aggregate used. Crushed granites can give the aesthetic appeal of granite paving without the cost and maintenance of granite slabs or pavers. Crushed glass can add glimmer to a water feature or patio. And even seashells can add the resort feel to an ocean-side getaway. The size of aggregate can also vary the color; whether you just have the sand exposed or if you go deeper can all have an impact on color.

DESIGNING WITH CONCRETE

Step 10 - Textures

Since we're talking about exterior concrete, I'm going to stick with exterior finishes. There are some areas of the country where smoother finishes may be applicable, but in Colorado we need to consider all weather conditions, so the textures I mention here are with that mindset. Let's start with the basics.

> **BUDGET IMPACTS:**
> - Finishes vary in costs, but typically increase in this order:
>   - Broom finish
>   - Exposed aggregate
>   - Stamped concrete
>   - Custom aggregates
>   - Art in concrete

DESIGNING WITH CONCRETE

Broom finish

This is the most common finish seen on city sidewalks and any exterior concrete without a direct specification. Typically the concrete is placed and then broom finished perpendicular to traffic flow. There are a couple variations to the traditional broom finish which can also be decorative. The broom can have alternating finishes; meaning it can go one direction in one square, then switch directions in the next. You can also have a swirl finish in which the broom goes in more of a radial sweeping motion. This finish is similar to a sweat finish. Broom finish can be decorative. However, a danger of broom finish, in my opinion, is that it can appear to be painted concrete with the wrong integral color (some pinks and yellows). Another danger is that the broom finish starts to wear off over time and it can become slick with no texture. In a directional broom finish, you also have the danger of creating directional slipping if used in a wet area, like around a pool.

Exposed finish

I mentioned this one earlier in colors, because it is by far my favorite with a multitude of color and texture options. There are shallow etches which just take the very cream off the surface. A favorite in Colorado is the sand finish. Sand finish creates a consistent finish across the surface while exposing the sand. This is an ideal finish because local sand can be beautiful, it provides consistent color and texture across the surface, and it provides great traction without being too rough. It is commonly used in walkways, pool decks, splash pads, heavily trafficked outdoor shopping malls, and every day paving. It wears beautifully since it is pre-aged by taking the top layer of cement off of the surface and providing the more durable sand as the walking surface.

But also making a re-appearance is the traditional chunkier exposed aggregate. Some of this trend is re-emerging due to the introduction of other materials, either added to the concrete mix, or seeded into the surface. The variety in color and texture is only limited to the materials available to you (and their ability to be mixed with the chemistry of concrete).

Some regions have better sand than others. Some states have to import aggregates while some manufacture them. Ask for samples or mockups to determine if it is the right choice for your area.

Stamped concrete

Some people love stamped concrete, some people despise it. However, stamped concrete has its place and can be versatile. Stamped concrete gives the durability of concrete while giving the character and texture of stone of other mediums. One reason people don't like it is because it's "fake" or trying to be something it isn't. Perhaps, but that is also the beauty of stamped concrete - it takes something as durable as concrete and can be formed, imprinted and colored to take on a whole new character. One of my personal favorites is a boardwalk stamp.

Given the right coloration and technique, you can have a faux wood concrete path that will never give you splinters! For non-vehicular concrete, stamped concrete consists of color hardener concrete coated with release agent and then imprinted with the desired texture or pattern. The concrete is first placed. While the concrete is still wet, a powdered color hardener is broadcast across the surface in a fashion similar to feeding chickens. The color hardener is your base and primary color. Color hardener not only adds pigment to the surface, it makes the surface more durable - hence the "hardener" in the name. After the color hardener is placed and troweled into the surface, a release agent is either spray applied (if liquid) or broadcasted on (if powder) over the top of the color hardener. The release agent serves two purposes. First, it allows the stamping tools to "release" from the concrete, giving a good clean imprint. Second, if tinted, it can provide an antiquing effect. I personally recommend using a colored release agent in a darker shade than the color hardener. The release agent typically settles in the crevices of the stamp, so it provides more dimension the the stamped texture and creates a more authentic look. If you like the cookie cutter look though, use a clear release agent for a mono-tone finish.

Stamped concrete opened the doors and eyes to the decorative concrete possibilities. Sure, integral color was fun, but once we saw the possibilities of stamped concrete, we knew so much more was possible! We started stamping concrete in the early 80's, and since that time, the world of decorative concrete opened up and let creativity flow. If concrete could be molded and shaped to look like stone, what else could be possible? A popular and timeless textured stamp is the slate texture. This texture can be done by itself, formed in smaller segments, saw cut patterns in it, or in a random stone type of stamped pattern.

Art in concrete

Many people may not think of concrete as an art form, but it is a wonderful medium for many expressions of art. Whether it is just through the shapes it creates or artwork that is applied to the concrete, concrete provides a strong artistic statement. A good carpenter can create extremely decorative concrete through creative formwork. A simple example of this is concrete countertops where sleek designs flow from clean forming, or dramatic shapes through unique uses of fabric or other unusual forming materials.

But when budget and imagination allow, concrete's artistic possibilities extend much further. Sandblasting, staining, overlays, airbrushing, and even mosaics can combine with concrete to create stunning and lasting masterpieces.

Decorative concrete is a passion of mine. It has unlimited possibilities for color, form and texture. The design potential is limitless. Every time I work with a landscape architect with a new idea or concept using concrete, I get excited about the possibilities. Every project is unique and concrete can be customized to meet the needs of every project out there. Concrete is exciting! People who don't understand the possibilities of concrete may think I'm crazy for getting so excited about concrete. I hope this book will give you a glimpse into the possibilities and start to get you excited about the medium as well. Concrete isn't just for city sidewalks any more, it can do so much more.

Step 11: Finding a Qualified Contractor

So, you think you know exactly what you want now that you have gone through all of the steps. Your dream can either become a reality now or become shattered with the reality of an inexperienced contractor. When comparing bids from decorative concrete contractors, it's important to know some qualifying factors. Ideally, you have already reached out to the contractor in the finish and color selection process. Many times people will come to me asking why some contractors cost more. Once I dive into the inclusions and explain the experience and processes – most of the time, everyone recognizes the value and understands that the lower price of someone else isn't always the same value as the dollar spent on a quality contractor. So what should you look for when selecting a decorative concrete contractor? Here is a list of what I would recommend:

1. **Experience** – Has the contractor installed something similar somewhere else? You don't want your project to be the first or the trial run. And do those other projects/instal-

lations live up to your expectations? Are the sawcuts and form lines straight? Does the concrete finish appear consistent? Does it match the design intent?

2   **Samples** – Can the contractor produce a small sample to show you the color and finish you are hoping for? If they can't produce something on a small scale that you like, chances are they can't produce it on a larger scale either.

3   **Mock-ups** – Small samples are great for selecting colors and finishes, but they are not representative of a true installation. If your project is large enough, it would be beneficial to require and pay for your decorative concrete contractor to install a full-scaled mock-up prior to the actual installation. The mock-up should be around 10'x10' and show the complexities your concrete project will have – everything from expansion, sawcuts, finishes, edges, walls, caulking, reinforcement, finishing, color, sealer, etc. If your project is not large enough to justify a mock-up, this is where the experienced qualifier comes into play again. Instead of a mock-up, request 3-5 other similar projects the decorative concrete contractor installed that you can physically visit to understand their capabilities.

4   **Details** – Now this can mean so many things, but it's the extra effort the contractor takes into consideration to make sure the project is complete and the best possible. Most of the details are in the minds of the craftsmen and just take the extra attention and thought. Some details crews should pay attention to include:

- Protecting adjacent surfaces during construction
- Laying out sawcuts before cutting them to ensure the best pattern both aesthetically and functionally
- Perform a final cleaning to ensure consistency in color and finish
- Seal the concrete – I recommend sealing all new concrete to help it through the first year of its life – concrete's most vulnerable timeframe
- Use edge grinders to finish a saw cut – many times the large blades on saws can't get to the very edge of what is being cut. So, rather than skipping the last bit,

or over cutting, our crews will use a smaller blade to bring it closer to the edge
- Clean up – seems simple, but cleaning up after themselves is a sign of a quality crew who takes pride in both their work and the project they are on

5. **Longevity** – Will the decorative concrete contractor be there next year, or in five years? You will want to choose a contractor who will be there for you, not only during that first year warranty period, but for years to come. You may have an addition down the road or a new need for decorative concrete. You also want to be confident that they will be there during the warranty period and stand behind their work.
6. **Responsiveness** – Do they answer your questions and concerns in a timely manner before, during and after construction?
7. **Loyalty** – Loyalty goes both ways. The relationship between you and your decorative concrete contractor should be one of trust. They may have additional resources and recommendations for your project and should always have your best interests in mind.
8. **Safety** – A decorative concrete contractor who respects the importance of safety is one you will want on your project. Safety for you, your clients, other workers, and themselves shows respect for everyone on and around the project and should be a requirement for anyone you hire.
9. **Resource** – A good decorative concrete contractor should be your expert in decorative concrete.

They should be able to make suggestions for your project as well as answer questions you may have. They should be able to show you options for your project, identify the best coloring techniques, give finish recommendations, help with budgets, provide samples, and even help with specifications.

Conclusion

By understanding the possibilities of concrete you can push the limits of design. The industry continues to change by people looking at the medium of concrete in a different light. When landscape architects approach me with a new challenge I get excited at the idea of taking another step further in the discovery of this material. I worked on a park with a team of talented landscape architects and they wanted bright purple and bright yellow concrete finished into a beautiful flower design. Rather than telling them it is impossible to make gray cement bright purple or yellow and is not cost efficient, we explored the possibilities together. To get either color vibrant with an integral color we would have to use white cement. White cement is not cheap, and this was a city project with a strict budget. Even if we did use a white cement base, the possibilities of getting a cost effective purple integral color is not practical. A bright blue alone is a couple thousand dollars per cubic yard last time I had it priced. It is not practical for a park budget. However, the design of bringing Colorado's native flowers into the design of the pavement was intriguing, so we kept digging. By working with one of my suppliers, we worked up some custom color hardeners. The result? Vibrant custom colors in the park's flower plaza. If you are a designer or an owner and have an idea, don't be afraid to ask about the possibilities. It takes all of us working together to keep this creative moment in going in the decorative concrete industry. So continue to dream and continue to build!

About The Author

Karen Keyes

Karen grew up in decorative concrete. By the time she was brought into the world, decorative concrete just started to get exciting. Concrete was just starting to get stamped and the concrete world was in for a drastic change. Her grandfather started a small concrete company in Denver and her father embraced the decorative possibilities from those concrete roots. Today, Karen collaborates with decorative concrete leaders across the nation to continue to advance the industry. Karen's passion and time is spent working with designers to help choose the appropriate concrete colors, finishes and details for their projects. Whether it's faux rocks or new concrete streetscaping, she finds the excitement in every project. Karen has 4 children - 2 boys and 2 girls, so projects that involve play and interaction of families is at the heart of what she enjoys. However, each project has an audience who has a specific need or requirement for their concrete, and finding the solution that is both functional and decorative is one of Karen's favorite parts of her job. You could say that concrete is in her blood, because it is in her heart, her history and her everyday living and breathing life.

She started The Art of Concrete in 2017 to push the envelope of concrete as an art form, after working most of her life prior to that in the decorative concrete family business. Karen has sat as the chairwoman of the Decorative Concrete Council, The Bomanite International Society, AGC Colorado's Diversity Council, and has served on both the ASCC and AGC Colorado Board of Directors. She is a LEED AP and focuses on building sustainably. The medium is always changing and new possibilities are discovered all the time. It's exciting and she hopes to share that excitement with the readers.

www.ingramcontent.com/pod-product-compliance
Lightning Source LLC
Chambersburg PA
CBHW040926190426
43197CB00033B/110